# I Can Make

# FANTASTIC

# FLIERS

by Kristina A. Holzweiss
and Amy Barth

# TABLE OF CONTENTS

GIANT BUBBLES

HOVERCRAFT

CATAPULT

# ARE YOU A MAKER?

Makers are inventors, artists, and builders. In this book, you will learn how to make three fantastic flying projects: giant bubbles, a hovercraft, and a catapult.

These projects look very different from each other. But they have something in common—**flight**. Flight is when something moves through the air.

Anyone can be a maker. You don't need fancy tools. You don't need to be a computer whiz. Are you creative and up for an adventure? Then you've got what it takes. Let's get started!

CATAPULT

GIANT BUBBLES

HOVERCRAFT

5

# MAKING CAN HAPPEN ANYWHERE!

You don't need a workshop to be a maker. You can make things in a classroom or on your kitchen floor. Project materials can be found around the house or at a craft shop.

You will need an adult's help with some steps. Like all inventors, you will try out your fliers. Then you will change your designs to make them even better.

# YOU CAN MAKE
# GIANT BUBBLES

Bubbles are liquid on the outside and have air on the inside. You can find bubbles in many different liquids. You can blow bubbles in a pool. You have probably seen bubbles in fizzy soda or soapy water.

Bubbles made of soapy water are special. They can float into the sky. You can make giant bubbles!

# HOW THESE SOAP BUBBLES WORK

## WAND

As the wand moves through the air, soapy water traps air inside. A bubble forms.

## INSIDE

The inside of a bubble is filled with air. That makes bubbles light enough to float.

## OUTSIDE

The outside is made of soap and water. Soap helps water stretch to form a bubble.

Bubbles are made from water. They will pop if the water evaporates. The bubble gets thinner and thinner until it pops.

Other things make bubbles pop, too. When a bubble lands on your finger or a blade of grass, it pops. Can you think of places where a bubble might last longer than others?

## DISCOVER MORE ABOUT
# EVAPORATION

In dry air, water evaporates. That means it changes from liquid to gas and floats away. On a hot day, water evaporates more quickly than on a cold day. Do you think bubbles last longer in warm or cold temperatures?

## INSTRUCTIONS

### YOU WILL NEED

- ☐ 6 cups water
- ☐ Plastic bucket
- ☐ ½ cup cornstarch
- ☐ Large spoon
- ☐ ½ cup dishwashing liquid
- ☐ 1 tablespoon baking powder
- ☐ 1 tablespoon glycerine (from the first aid aisle of a drug store)
- ☐ Scissors
- ☐ Spool of cotton string
- ☐ Two straight plastic drinking straws

**1**

Pour the water into the bucket. Add the cornstarch and stir until it dissolves.

**2**

Add the dishwashing liquid, baking powder, and glycerine to the bucket. Stir well, but don't make the mixture too sudsy.

et your bubble mix
it for 1 hour.

In the meantime,
make your wand.
Cut a piece of string
6 to 8 times longer
than a straw.

Thread the string
through both straws.
Tie the ends of the
string together to
make a loop.

## MAKE IT FLY

Transfer the bubble mixture to a
large, shallow container. Soak your
wand in the bubble mixture. Hold
one straw in each hand. Carefully
separate them to open the loop.
Wave the open loop slowly to make
a giant bubble.

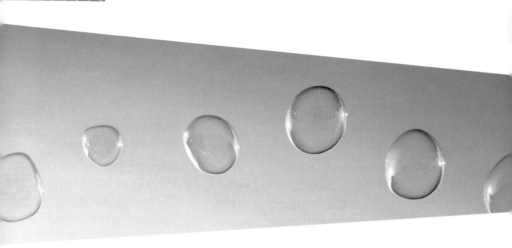

## TEST IT

How long do your giant bubbles last before they pop? Does moving your wand faster or slower through the air change the shape or size of the bubbles? What happens if you run while holding the wand to the side?

## CHANGE IT

····▶ Use a longer piece of string to make a bigger wand. Does this change the size of your bubbles?

····▶ Try adding more dishwashing liquid to the mixture. Does that change how long your bubbles last? Why do you think that is?

# YOU CAN MAKE A HOVERCRAFT

Hovercrafts are machines that glide on air. They hover over smooth surfaces like land, water, ice, or sand.

Hovercrafts might look like they are magically floating on the air. But there is a lot of science at work. A hovercraft blows air out from its underside. This pushes the craft up into the air.

# HOW A HOVERCRAFT WORKS

**FAN**
The fan directs air out of the bottom of the craft. The **force** of the air hitting the surface below causes the craft to rise.

**SKIRT**
The skirt helps trap air below the craft, so the cushion of air doesn't disappear.

**AIR CUSHION**
Hovercrafts float on a cushion of air.

A hovercraft works by gliding on an air cushion. Hovercrafts usually have a skirt surrounding the bottom of the machine. The skirt helps trap air below the craft. In this project, the CD is light enough that you do not need a skirt.

## DISCOVER MORE ABOUT
# AIR PRESSURE

Hovercrafts use air pressure to rise. Air **particles** bounce off each other and things around them. The force created by these particles is called air pressure.

When a hovercraft blows out air, the air pressure below it increases. When the force of this air pressure equals the weight of the craft, it will hover.

## INSTRUCTIONS

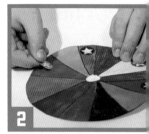

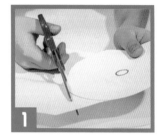

**1** Place the CD flat on the piece of paper. Trace around the outside and inside. Place the CD to the side. Cut out the inner and outer circles.

**2** Decorate the paper circle. Be as creative as possible!

| Use the glue stick to attach the circle to the top of the CD. Make sure the center holes line up. | Ask an adult for help using the hot glue gun. Attach the water bottle cap to the center of the top of the CD. | Blow up the balloon as big as you can. Twist and hold the end of the balloon so the air stays inside. |
|---|---|---|

Place your hovercraft on a flat surface, like a table or floor. Open the bottle top, and give the craft a gentle push.

Make sure the bottle cap is closed. Stretch the end of the balloon over the top of the bottle cap.

## TEST IT

Use a tape measure and a stopwatch to record how far and how long the hovercraft travels. Test the hovercraft over different surfaces, such as a wood floor, a pool of water, and a sandbox. On which surface does it hover the longest? Why do you think that is?

## CHANGE IT

····► Fill the balloon with more or less air. How does this affect how long your hovercraft hovers?

····► Try a different size bottle top, like one from a bottle of liquid dish soap.

····► Tape a strip of paper around the bottom of your CD to make a skirt. Does this change how well your craft works?

# YOU CAN MAKE
# A CATAPULT

A catapult is a machine that flings things into the air. It was invented to fight battles more than 2,000 years ago. Catapults could hurl heavy rocks into castles.

Today, catapults are used for fun. People build catapults to see how far they can hurl an object through the air. How far can your catapult send things flying?

# HOW A CATAPULT WORKS

## PROJECTILE

A projectile is an object that is thrown into the air.

## FULCRUM

The arm balances on the fulcrum. Together the arm and fulcrum form a lever, which helps the catapult toss heavy objects.

## ARM

When you push down on the arm, you load it with energy. When you let go, this energy is transferred to the launched object. It flies through the air.

Ancient Greeks and Romans used catapults to launch stones toward their enemies. The stones follow a **trajectory**, or path, as they fly. The distance a stone travels depends on the angle of the catapult's arm and how far the arm is pushed down. You can make a catapult that can hit a far-off target! (But don't hit anyone!)

# LEVERS

Levers are simple machines that help people move heavy objects. On a catapult, the arm and the fulcrum hinge together to make a lever. The farther you can push down the arm, the farther the object will fly!

## YOU WILL NEED

- ☐ Eight wide craft sticks
- ☐ Markers, crayons, colored pencils, stickers
- ☐ Four or more rubber bands
- ☐ Hot glue gun
- ☐ Hot glue sticks
- ☐ Plastic bottle cap

## INSTRUCTIONS

**1**

Decorate the craft sticks. Stack six on top of each other. Wrap a rubber band around both ends of the stack. This is stack A. Place it to the side.

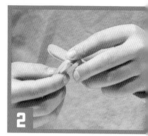

**2**

Stack the remaining two craft sticks together. Wrap a rubber band around one end of the stack. This is stack B.

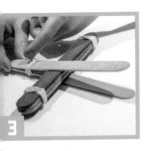

**3**

Separate the two craft sticks at the open end of stack B. Slide stack A into the space between the two sticks.

**4**

Wrap a rubber band around both stacks.

**5**

Ask an adult for help using the hot glue gun. Attach the plastic bottle cap to the end of the top craft stick. The inside of the bottle cap should face up.

## MAKE IT FLY

Place your catapult on a flat surface. Place a button or pom-pom in the bottle cap. Push the cap down and let go. Use a tape measure or yardstick to measure how far the button or pom-pom flew.

## TEST IT

Try hurling different objects through the air.
Try a pebble, a penny, or a marshmallow. Use a
tape measure to measure how far each object flies.
What flew the farthest? Why do you think that is?

## CHANGE IT

····▶ Add more craft sticks to stack A to change the angle of your catapult's arm. Does that change how far the button flies?

····▶ Use a plastic spoon instead of a craft stick to make the arm of your catapult longer and more flexible. What happens?

····▶ Use lightweight blocks to build a tower near your catapult. Hurl different objects at the tower to knock it down. What works best?

# MASTERS OF FLIGHT

## GALILEO GALILEI

Galileo Galilei was a famous mathematician, inventor, and scientist. He was born in Pisa, Italy, in 1564. Galileo studied the path of objects as they flew through the air. Galileo figured out the math behind an object's trajectory, or flight path.

## IGOR SIKORSKY

Igor Sikorsky invented the helicopter. Sikorsky was born in Russia in 1889 and moved to the United States in 1919. He made a small helicopter that could rise into the air when he was just 12. In 1939, his first full-size helicopter took flight at Stratford, Connecticut.

25

## ORVILLE WRIGHT
## WILBUR WRIGHT

## CHARLES LINDBERGH

The first airplane took flight in 1903 in North Carolina. It was built by brothers Orville and Wilbur Wright. The Wright brothers tested airplanes for years before they built one that took off and landed safely.

Charles Lindbergh was born in 1902. He was the first person to fly solo across the Atlantic Ocean. In 1927, he took off near New York City and landed near Paris, France. The trip was more than 3,600 miles (5,794 km).

## SALLY RIDE

**Sally Ride** was born
in 1951. In 1983,
she became the first
American woman
to fly in space. She flew
aboard the *Challenger*
space shuttle. Ride's
job was to operate the
shuttle's robotic arm.

# TIMELINE:

## MACHINES THAT FLY

**Check out this timeline about some of the coolest fliers ever made.**

### 1783
Joseph and Jacques Montgolfier of France invent the hot air balloon.

### 1903
The Wright brothers make the first ever recorded flight.

### 1939
The first helicopter takes off.

### 1947
The first supersonic plane takes flight. It travels more than twice as fast as a passenger jet.

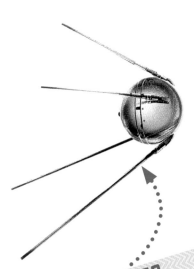

## 2016
First private space flights take off, carrying supplies to the International Space Station.

## 1969
American astronauts Neil Armstrong and Buzz Aldrin become the first people to walk on the moon.

## 1957
*Sputnik*, a Russian satellite, is the first object carried into space aboard a rocket.

## 1950s
Christopher Cockerell of England invents the hovercraft.

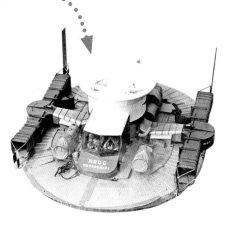

**Flight** *(flite)*

The act or manner of flying, or the ability to fly.

**Force** *(fors)*

Any action that produces, stops, or changes the shape or the movement of an object.

**Particles** *(pahr-ti-kuhls)*

Extremely small pieces or amounts of something.

**Trajectory** *(truh-jek-tuh-ree)*

The path that something follows through space.

## ABOUT THE AUTHORS

**Kristina A. Holzweiss** was selected by School Library Journal as the School Librarian of the Year in 2015. She is the Founder of SLIME—Students of Long Island Maker Expo and the President of Long Island LEADS, a nonprofit organization to promote STEAM education and the maker movement. In her free time, Kristina enjoys making memories with her husband, Mike, and their three children, Tyler, Riley, and Lexy.

**Amy Barth** is a writer and editor specializing in science content for kids in elementary through high school. She writes about robots, penguins, volcanoes, and beyond! She lives in Los Angeles, California.

Scholastic Library Publishing wants to especially thank Kristina A. Holzweiss, Bay Shore Middle School, and all the kids who worked as models in these books for their time and generosity.

Library of Congress Cataloging-in-Publication Data

Names: Holzweiss, Kristina A., author. | Barth, Amy, 1984– author.
Title: I Can Make Fantastic Fliers/by Kristina A. Holzweiss and Amy Barth.
Description: New York, NY: Children's Press, an imprint of Scholastic Inc., 2018. | Series: Rookie star makerspace projects | Includes index.
Identifiers: LCCN 2016053241 | ISBN 9780531234129 (library binding) | ISBN 9780531238813 (pbk.)
Subjects: LCSH: Bubbles—Juvenile literature. | Ground-effect machines—Juvenile literature. | Catapult—Juvenile literature. | Handicraft—Juvenile literature.
Classification: LCC QC183 .H756 2018 | DDC 745.592—dc23
LC record available at https://lccn.loc.gov/2016053241

Design: Judith Christ-Lafond & Anna Tunick Tabachnik
Text: Kristina A. Holzweiss & Amy Barth
© 2018 Scholastic Inc.

All rights reserved. Published in 2018 by Children's Press, an imprint of Scholastic Inc.
Printed in China 62
SCHOLASTIC, CHILDREN'S PRESS and associated logos are trademarks and/or registered trademarks of Scholastic Inc., 557 Broadway, New York, NY 10012.

1 2 3 4 5 6 7 8 9 10 R 27 26 25 24 23 22 21 20 19 18

Photos ©: back cover left: panic_attack/iStockphoto; 2 left and throughout: Viorika/iStockphoto; 6 scissors: fotomy/iStockphoto; 6 crayons: Charles Brutlag/Dreamstime; 6 tape: Carolyn Franks/Dreamstime; 6 glue gun: Nilsz/Dreamstime; 6 markers: Floortje/Getty Images; 6 straws: Olga Dubravina/Shutterstock; 6 marble: David Arky/Getty Images; 6 CD: Roman Sigaev/Shutterstock; 6 bottle cap: Mrs_ya/Shutterstock; 6 pencil: antomanio/iStockphoto; 7: AndreasKermann/iStockphoto; 9 bowl: Stocksearch/Alamy Images; 9 background and throughout: Hughstoneian/Dreamstime; 10 left: somchaij/Shutterstock; 14: stefann11/iStockphoto; 15 center: mrs/Getty Images; 16 bottle cap: pbombaert/Shutterstock; 18 left: AnatolyM/iStockphoto; 18 right: pongam/iStockphoto; 18 center: Robert Cocquyt/Dreamstime; 20: jgroup/iStockphoto; 21 apples: Xerography/Shutterstock; 24 marshmallow: subjug/iStockphoto; 25 left: Hulton Achive/Getty Images; 25 right: Keystone-France/Gamma-Keystone/Getty Images; 25 center: IgorGolovniov/Shutterstock; 26 top left: Popperfoto/Getty Images; 26 bottom left: Apic/Getty Images; 26 top right: Keystone-France/Gamma-Keystone/Getty Images; 26 bottom center: Underwood Archives/Getty Images; 26 bottom right: Bettmann/Getty Images; 27 left: Bettmann/Getty Images; 27 right: Bettmann/Getty Images; 28 left: Chris Lyon/Getty Images; 28 center: Mary Evans/Grenville Collins Postcard Collection/age fotostock; 28 bottom right: Everett Collection/Superstock, Inc.; 28 top right: Underwood Archives/Getty Images; 29 bottom left: Evening Standard/Getty Images; 29 top left: RFStock/iStockphoto; 29 top center: Time & Life Pictures/Getty Images; 29 top right: Ben Cooper/Getty Images; 29 bottom right: Kevork Djansezian/Getty Images; 30 top: Keystone-France/Gamma-Keystone/Getty Images; 30 bottom: jgroup/iStockphoto; 30 center bottom: Stocksearch/Alamy Images.

All instructional images by Jennifer A. Uihlein.
All other images by Bianca Alexis Photography.